Into the Next Millennium

Exploration

Deborah Cannarella
Jane Fournier

The Rourke Press
Vero Beach, Florida

Photo credits

All images © copyright: AP/Wide World Photos, pp. 11 middle, 13 bottom left, 16 top, 17 bottom; California Association for Research in Astronomy and the W.M. Keck Observatory, p. 22 top (Andrew Perala); Corbis, p. 9 top, 12 top, 19 top, 23 top; Corbis/Bettman, pp. 6 bottom, 7 top and bottom, 9 bottom, 10 bottom, 14 bottom, 20 top, 21 bottom; Hulton Getty Images, p. 6 top; Mobile Technology Company, p. 25 top and 26 bottom, 28 top; NASA, pp. 21 top, 29 bottom, 30 top and bottom; NOAA-NURC-UNCW, p. 25 bottom and 31 bottom; North Wind Picture Archives, pp. 10 top; Office of Instructional Resources, University of Florida, p. 15 top; PhotoDisc, p. 18 bottom right; Seth Shostak, p. 31 top; Stock Montage, Inc., pp. 4 bottom and 8 top (Newberry Library), 4–5 and 8 bottom, 4 top and 11 top, 11 bottom, 1 and 18 bottom left, 4 middle and 19 bottom, 20 bottom; Tom and Therisa Stack, p. 22 bottom; TSADO/GSFC/Tom Stack & Associates, pp. 23 bottom, 25 middle and 27; TSADO/NASA/Tom Stack & Associates, p. 24–25 and 28 bottom, 29 top; UPI/Corbis-Bettmann, pp. 12 bottom, 13 top, 13 bottom right, 14 top, 15 bottom, 16 bottom, 17 top, 18 top; Woods Hole Oceanographic Institution, p. 26 top. All cover and introduction page images PhotoDisc.

Printed in the United States of America

An Editorial Directions Book
Book design and production by Criscola Design

Library of Congress Cataloging-in-Publication Data

Cannarella, Deborah.
Exploration / Deborah Cannarella, Jane Fournier.
p. cm. - (Into the next millennium)
Includes index.
Summary : Describes our explorations of land, sea, and space throughout history and the devices and methods used.
ISBN 1-57103-273-8
1. Discoveries in geography Juvenile literature. [1. Discoveries in geography. 2. Outer space-Exploration.] I. Fournier, Jane, 1955- . II. Title. III. Series.
G175.C34 1999
910'.9-dc21 99-27214
CIP

Introduction

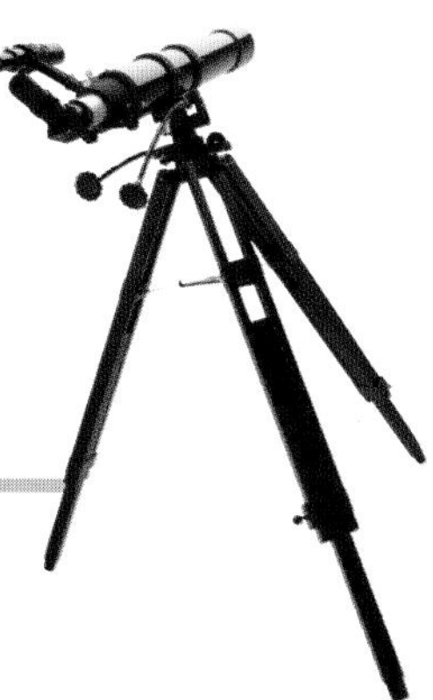

The history of the human race is a story of great discoveries and amazing achievements. Since ancient times, people have found creative solutions to problems, met impossible challenges, and turned visions into reality. Each of these remarkable people—and each of their contributions—changed the world they lived in forever. Together, they created the world we know and live in today.

The six books in this series—*Medicine, Transportation, Communication, Exploration, Engineering,* and *Sports*—present a timeline of the great discoveries and inventions that have shaped our world. As you travel from ancient to modern times, you will discover the many ways in which people have worked to heal sickness, shape materials, share information, explore strange places, and achieve new goals. Although they worked with many different tools, their goal was always the same: to improve our quality of life.

As we enter the twenty-first century, we will continue to build on what each generation of people before us has created and discovered. With the knowledge they have given us, we will discover new ways to build, heal, communicate, discover, and achieve. We will continue to change the world in ways we can only begin to imagine.

FRANCIA
MAR D
Hispanis :
AMERICA
P A C I

*From the **Past**...*

2600 B.C.

A compass is a device for determining direction. In a **magnetic compass,** a piece of magnetic iron—called lodestone—aligns with the natural magnetic fields of Earth. The magnetic compass may first have been used in ancient China as early as 2600 B.C. Sailors used compasses to check the direction of the wind and to guide their ships. The figure on this Chinese magnetic chariot points south.

The oldest known map was drawn on a clay brick called a tablet in Babylonia (now part of Iraq) in about 2500 B.C. It shows a settlement in a valley surrounded by mountains.

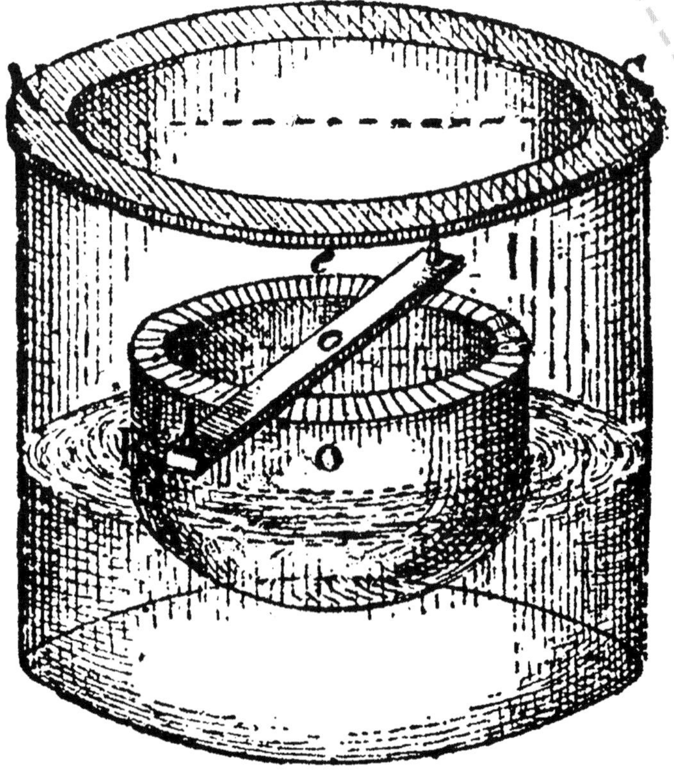

1269

Peter Peregrinus of Maricourt was the first to write about how magnets work. He also described the **floating mariner's compass.** In a floating compass, a bar of magnetic iron floats on a piece of cork or straw in a bowl of water. The bar turns to align with Earth's magnetic field.

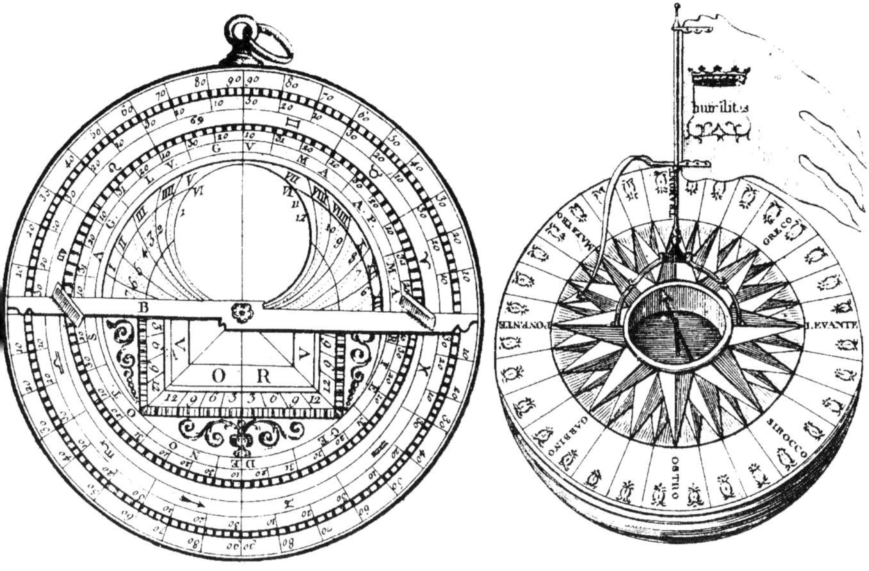

1450

An **astrolabe** (left) measures the angle of the Sun, Moon, or a star above Earth's horizon. Sailors used it to tell the time of day and their position at sea. The earliest astrolabe dates from the ninth century. The magnetic needle of the mariner's compass (right) points to one of the 32 directions marked on the compass card.

Martin Behaim of Portugal created the first globe of Earth in 1492, the year Columbus sailed to North America. The New World's name, America, first appeared on a map made by Martin Waldseemüller in 1507—to honor the Italian explorer Amerigo Vespucci.

1500

Artist and inventor Leonardo da Vinci designed several **diving suits** that would allow a person to explore the ocean's depths. One design included a leather helmet with spikes to protect the diver from undersea monsters! In the design at right, a crush-proof air chamber is attached to the diver's chest so that the diver can swim freely underwater—without needing to breathe through long hoses.

1569

Gerardus Mercator created the **Mercator map** to help sailors plan routes across long distances. His system presented the round Earth on a flat piece of paper. To show distances and positions, he drew straight lines that represented the lines of longitude and latitude. Mercator's map of the world, made in 1569, made him famous. His system is still used today.

In 1519, Ferdinand Magellan of Spain set sail for Asia with five ships. In 1522, his ship *Victoria* returned to Spain—the only one to make the first trip around the world.

1608

Telescopes similar to binoculars were invented by a Dutch eyeglass maker in 1608. In 1609, Galileo Galilei built the **first telescope** designed to examine stars and planets. He was the first to see the moons of Jupiter and the mountains and valleys on the surface of Earth's moon. In 1668, Sir Isaac Newton developed the first reflecting telescope, which used a mirror instead of two lenses.

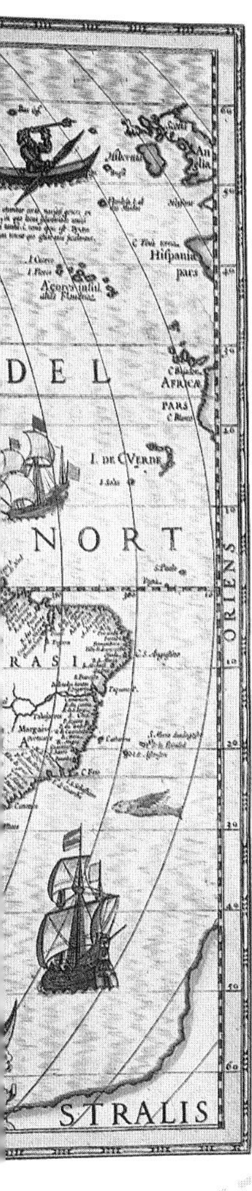

1690

During the seventeenth century, people explored the ocean in **diving bells.** Divers could leave these bell-shaped containers for short periods. Then, they returned to the bell to breathe the air trapped inside. In 1690, Edmond Halley—discoverer of Halley's Comet—built an improved version of the diving bell. His design included two barrels of extra air and a system for refilling the bell, which allowed divers to stay underwater for longer periods.

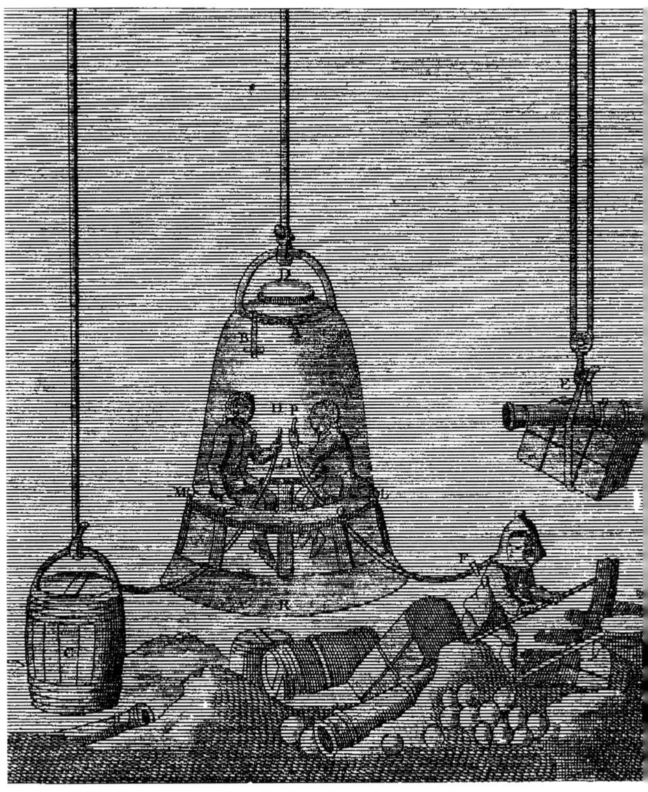

Early people simply held their breath to explore underwater. The ancient Greeks and Romans dove in search of pearls, sponges, and shells. In about 1300, divers in the Persian Gulf wore goggles made of polished clear tortoise shell.

1731

John Hadley and Thomas Godfrey invented the **octant** to help sailors determine their position at sea. It had two mirrors, a telescope, and an arc with a series of measurements. A person aligned the reflection of the Sun or a star with Earth's horizon and measured the angle. A larger, improved version of the octant, called a sextant, was developed later in the century.

1820

People who measure and record areas of land are called surveyors. Early surveyors used a chain to measure distances and a compass to measure direction. In the early 1800s, these tools were replaced by instruments such as the **theodolite.** A theodolite has a telescope that can move horizontally (from side to side) and vertically (up and down). It is also used to measure angles for mapmaking.

Maria Mitchell was the first professional woman astronomer in the United States. She discovered a comet on October 1, 1847.

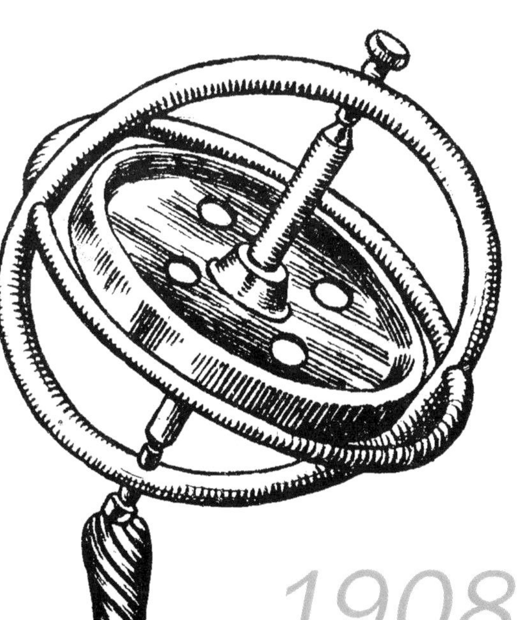

In 1763, John Harrison won a worldwide contest that had lasted almost 50 years. He invented the chronometer, the first clock that could keep accurate time at sea. This clock allowed sailors to calculate their ship's longitude and stay on course.

1908

A gyroscope is a free-moving wheel that is set in a frame. The wheel in a **gyrocompass** indicates the direction in which a ship, plane, or submarine is moving or leaning. In 1909, Elmer A. Sperry built the first automatic pilot to keep an aircraft on course. His device relied on the same method used in the gyrocompass.

1909

Robert Edwin Peary is known as the first explorer to reach the **North Pole**—but he may actually have been 30 to 60 miles (48 to 96 km) away. The journal he kept during his trip showed he might have made mistakes in navigation and record keeping. For example, his chronometer, a clock used to determine location, was 10 minutes fast!

The first confirmed trip by land to the North Pole was by Ralph Plaisted, who arrived there by snowmobile in 1968.

1911

When Roald Amundsen heard that Robert Peary had reached the North Pole, he decided to head to the **South Pole.** Amundsen and his crew traveled in four sleds pulled by 52 dogs. They arrived on December 14, 1911. Five weeks later, Robert Scott and his men—who had chosen a more difficult route and used ponies instead of dogs to pull the sleds—found the Norwegian flag that Amundsen and his crew had left behind.

1918

The word *sonar* stands for "**so**und **na**vigation **r**anging." **Sonar** is a technique for determining the position of underwater objects by measuring sound waves. Sonar has been used to locate icebergs, schools of fish, submarines, torpedoes, and sunken ships. It is also used to measure the ocean's depth and to map the surface of the ocean floor.

The first rockets were made in China nearly 1,000 years ago. They were attached to arrows for use in battle. The German V-2 war rocket, made in 1942, was the first rocket powerful enough to reach space. In 1957, a Soviet rocket launched the first space satellite.

1926

As a young man, Robert Goddard dreamed of making a device that had the "*possibility* of ascending to Mars." In 1914, he began designing **rocket engines.** In 1926, he launched the first rocket that had an engine that burned liquid fuel. By 1930, one of his rockets reached 2,000 feet (610 m), traveling 500 miles (804 km) per hour. In 1935, he shot the first rocket to travel faster than the speed of sound—about 1,087 feet (331 m) per second.

1925

The word *radar* stands for "**ra**dio **d**etecting **a**nd **r**anging." **Radar** is a system for determining the position and distance of an object by measuring radio waves. Today, radar is an important navigational tool for planes and ships. It is also used for weather prediction and for space exploration.

1929

In 1928, explorer **Richard Byrd** sailed to Little America, a base in the Antarctic. A year later, he and his pilot flew from there to the South Pole and back again. Byrd was the first person to fly to both the North Pole (in 1926) and the South Pole. He later led more trips to the frozen regions of the Antarctic to study the weather, geology, and geography.

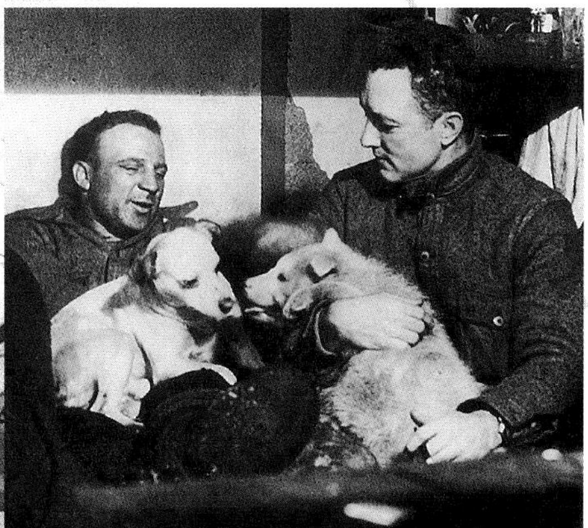

1934

In 1934, William Beebe and Otis Barton descended a record 3,028 feet (924 m) into the ocean near Bermuda in a **bathysphere.** The bathysphere, which was invented by Barton, is a hollow, steel ball that is lowered into the water on a steel cable that is attached to a ship.

The British *Challenger* was the first ship whose mission was to explore the ocean. From 1872 to 1876, it covered almost 70,000 nautical miles (113,000 km). Its scientists made depth soundings (measurements) of the ocean and discovered many types of sea creatures.

1937

A **radio telescope** gathers information about objects in space. It has a large reflector, or dish, that collects the natural radio waves of stars, planets, and other bodies. An antenna translates the radio waves into electric signals, which are recorded by a computer. The first radio telescope was built by Grote Reber.

Aerial photography provides a way to learn more about Earth's surface. Cameras attached to aircraft take a series of pictures. Maps and models are then made from the photographs. Aerial photographs provide information about land masses, bodies of water, and even weather patterns. Cameras mounted on rockets, satellites, or other spacecraft can photograph regions of outer space.

Before satellites, balloons were used to explore Earth's atmosphere and the edges of outer space. In 1932, Auguste Piccard rose about 55,000 feet (16,916 m) in a huge balloon to study cosmic rays.

1943

Jacques-Yves Cousteau and Emile Gagnan invented the **aqualung.** This simple device provided a supply of air as a diver moved underwater. In 1947, Frédéric Dumas made a record dive with the aqualung to 307 feet (94 m). Cousteau developed many more techniques for undersea exploration and made many voyages with his research ship *Calypso.*

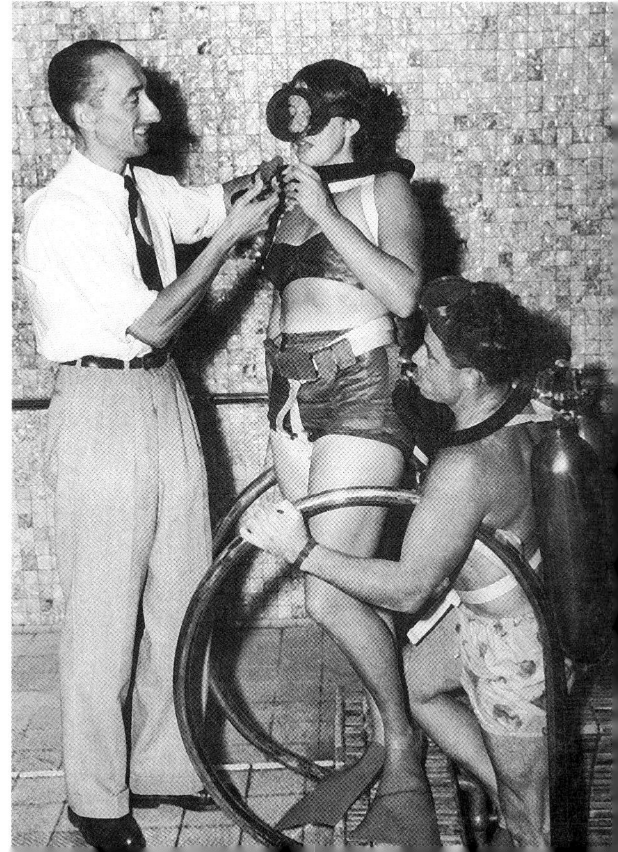

1948

In 1948, balloonist Auguste Piccard designed a deep-sea diving ship called a **bathyscaphe.** It could travel deeper into the ocean than the bathysphere. In 1953, Piccard and his son, Jacques, reached a depth of 10,300 feet (3,150 m) in the *Trieste.*

***Luna 1* was launched in 1959. It was the first artificial craft to fly out of the field of Earth's gravity, past the Moon, and orbit the Sun.**

***Mariner 10* was the first spacecraft to study two planets—delivering close-up photographs of Venus in 1974 and of Mercury in 1974 and 1975.**

1957

Sputnik 1 was the **first artificial satellite** launched into orbit. It circled Earth every 96 minutes at a speed of 18,000 mph (29,000 kph). It traveled as far as 584 miles (942 km) away from the planet and sent back radio signals. A dog named Laika—a passenger on *Sputnik 2*—became the first traveler in space.

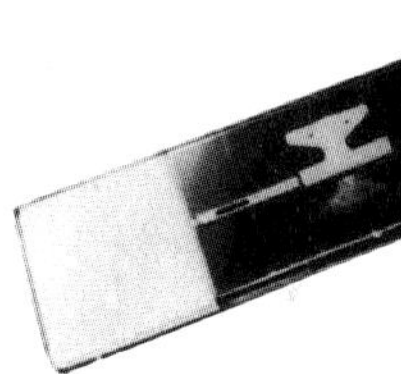

1961

Yury Gagarin, of the Soviet Air Force, was the **first person to travel in space.** He circled Earth once, traveling for 1 hour 29 minutes at a speed of more than 17,000 miles (27,400 km) per hour. *Vostok 1* traveled about 200 miles (322 km) above the Earth.

John H. Glenn Jr., a test pilot for the U.S. Marines, was the first American to orbit Earth. In 1962, he circled the planet three times in less than five hours in *Friendship 7.* In 1998, at age seventy-seven, John Glenn traveled in Earth's orbit for nine days on the space shuttle *Discovery.* He was the oldest person ever to travel in space.

1962

A space probe is a device sent into outer space to gather information. The U.S. space probe *Mariner 2* sent information about Venus back to Earth. The probe traveled within 22,000 miles (13,700 km) of Venus. *Mariner 5,* launched in 1967, traveled within 2,500 miles (1,500 km) of the planet. Later Mariner probes took photographs of Mars and Mercury.

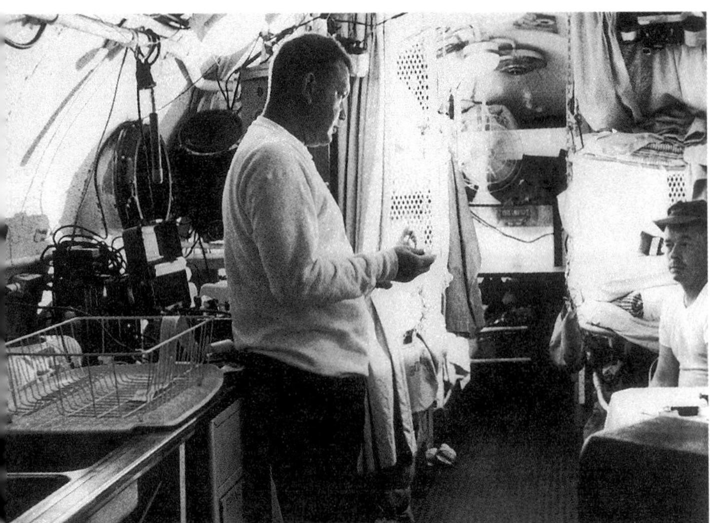

1964

The mission of the U.S. Navy's program **Sealab** was to study how humans could live beneath the ocean's surface. The "aquanauts" lived on the ocean floor about 26 miles (42 km) off Bermuda in 193 feet (59 m) of water. *Sealab II* began tests in 1965 off the coast of California. One of the aquanauts on board was former astronaut Scott Carpenter.

1969

Apollo 11 was the first manned spacecraft to **land on the Moon.** Astronaut Neil A. Armstrong was the first person ever to set foot on the surface of the Moon. By 1972, U.S. astronauts had made five more landings on the Moon.

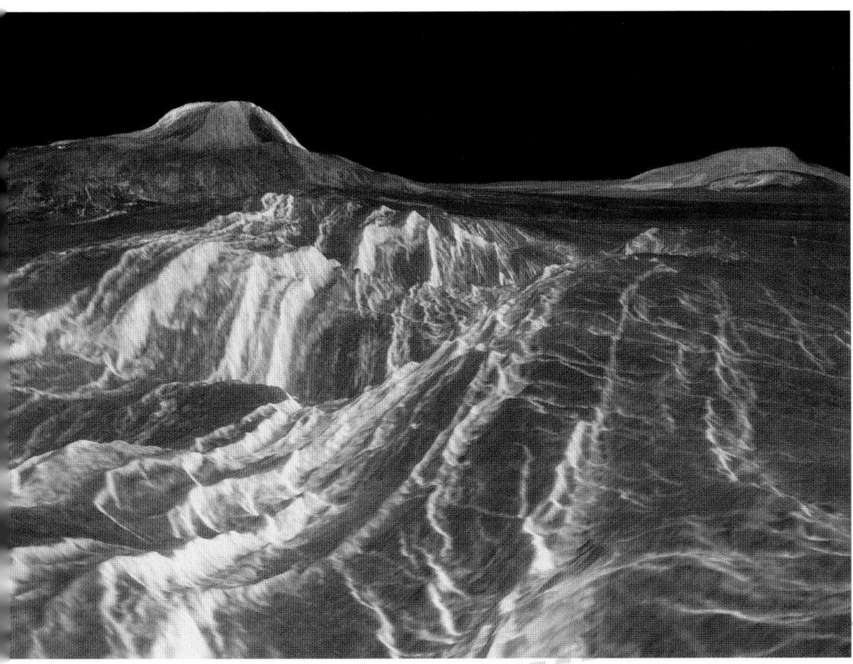

1970

The Soviet spacecraft *Venera 7* was the first craft to **land on Venus.** It was the first successful landing on another planet. *Mariner 10* sent back the first close-up photographs of the planet in 1974. *Venera 9* landed on Venus in 1975 and provided close-up photographs of the planet's surface.

1973

The United States established the **first space station** in 1973. The satellite was launched into Earth's orbit by rocket. Three teams of astronauts made trips to *Skylab* to conduct research—spending a total of 171 days in space. *Skylab* wandered from its orbit and fell into the Earth's atmosphere in 1979.

In 1962, Jacques-Yves Cousteau began an underwater living experiment called the Conshelf (Continental Shelf) program. "Oceanauts" lived and worked underwater for extended periods of time.

1973

Pioneer 10 was the first space probe to explore the **planet Jupiter** in 1973. The information it sent to scientists proved that Jupiter has a magnetic tail about 500 million miles (800 million km) long. *Pioneer 10* flew within 81,000 miles (130,000 km) of the planet. *Pioneer 11,* launched in 1973, reached Saturn in 1974. This probe discovered two more of Saturn's rings.

In 1985, French and American explorers—led by Robert Ballard and Jean-Louis Michel—dove to find the ship *Titanic,* which had sunk in the North Atlantic in 1912. *Argo,* a small submarine with lights and cameras helped the crew find the remains of the sunken ship.

1976

In 1975, the United States launched two probes into the orbit of the **planet Mars.** The next year, *Viking 1* and *Viking 2* touched down on the surface to gather information. They measured the weather and tested the soil for life forms—but none was found. The *Vikings* sent color photographs of large areas of the planet's surface back to Earth.

1986

In 1986, the Soviet Union launched the space station *Mir,* which was designed to be a **permanent space laboratory.** In 1991, the United States joined forces with Russia in the space-station program. In 1995, American astronaut Norman E. Thagard spent almost four months on the space station *Mir.*

***SEASAT,* launched in 1978, was the first satellite designed to explore the oceans. To gather data, it used a radar system called SAR (Synthetic Aperture Radar).**

1990

The **Hubble Space Telescope** is a reflecting telescope that orbits about 370 miles (600 km) above Earth. The U.S. space shuttle *Discovery* launched the telescope into space. The Hubble takes photographs of galaxies, planets, and other objects in space. It has provided scientists with information about black holes and Pluto, the most distant planet in the solar system.

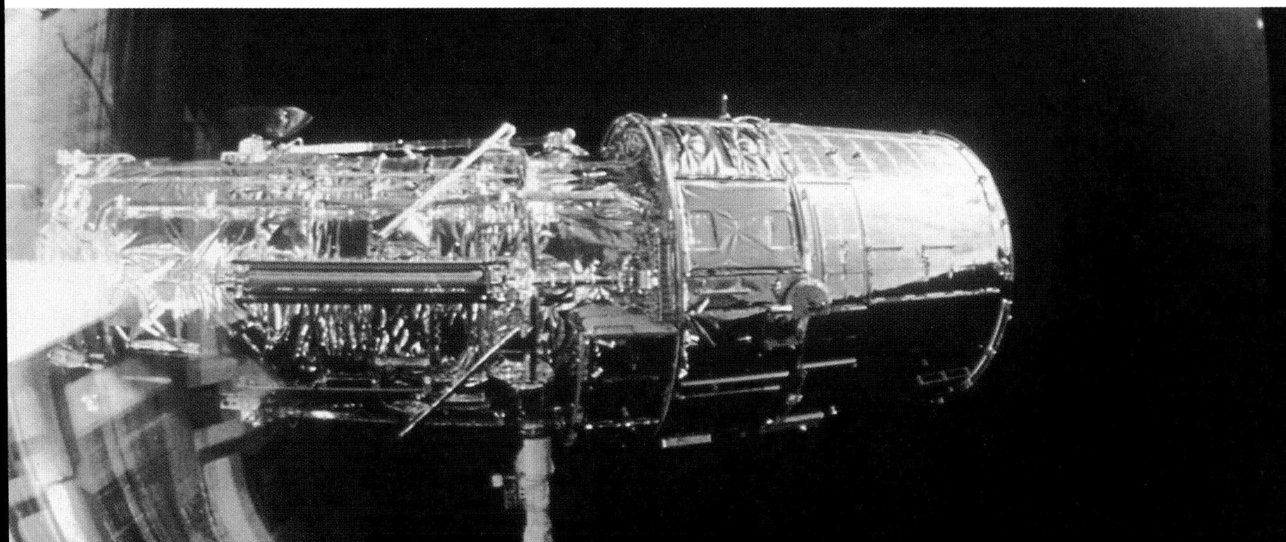

1992

The Keck Telescope is the **largest reflecting telescope** in the world. Its large, multiple mirrors collect light waves and infrared (heat) rays given off by objects in space. Scientists study distant galaxies with this powerful telescope, which is located on Mauna Kea, a mountain on the island of Hawaii.

The ice caps at the North and South Poles are the areas of Earth that are most sensitive to global climate change. Scientists are studying whether the shrinking of the arctic and Antarctic caps is caused by human pollution or is part of a natural cycle.

The Hubble Space Telescope can see more clearly, but the Keck telescope can see farther than any other telescope in the world. A telescope's power is measured by its ability to gather light. Keck's mirrors gather 17 times more light than the Hubble.

1993

Aquarius is the world's leading **undersea research laboratory.** Scientists live and work underwater for 10-day periods, studying the coral reefs off the coast of Florida. They spend six to nine hours a day in the water—sometimes even exploring at night. While inside the living chamber, the crew can watch the sea life through the portholes (windows).

1995

The polar regions provide scientists with valuable information—not only about Earth, but also about the rest of the solar system. As of 1995, 28 nations were conducting **polar research** in field programs in Antarctica—more than ever before.

Polar organisms thrive under the ice because of their natural "antifreeze." Scientists wonder if similar life forms may exist under the ice that covers Europa, one of Jupiter's moons.

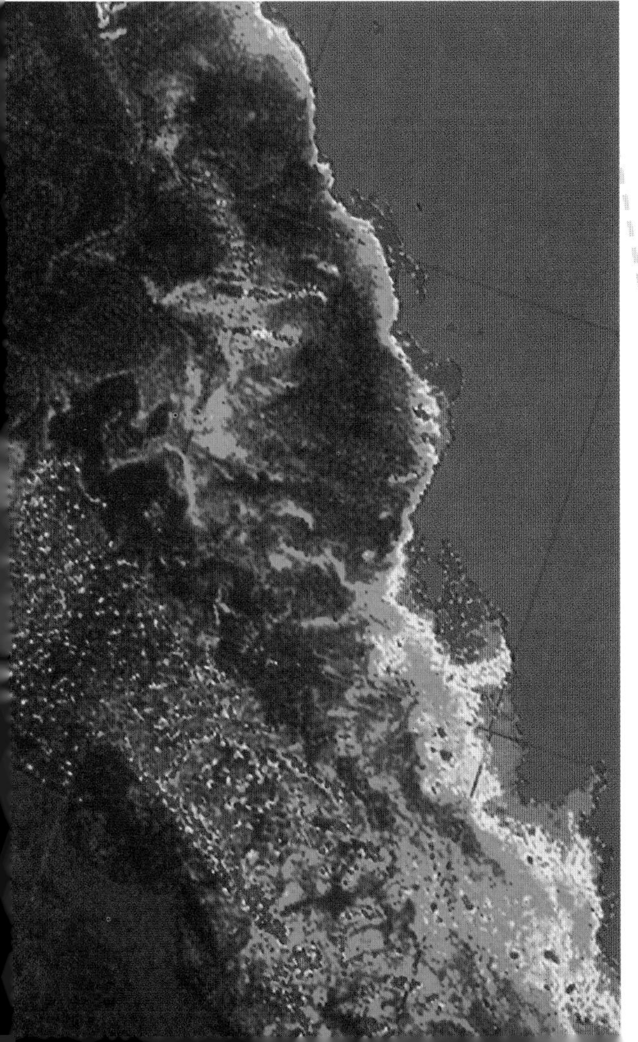

1997

The Goddard Space Flight Center's satellite ***SeaStar*** has an instrument on board called SeaWiFS. From space, this instrument records the "ocean color." Ocean color—which measures how much marine plant life is in the water—helps scientists understand the changes caused by global warming. The SeaWiFS Mission is part of the Mission to Planet Earth (MTPE), designed to study Earth from space.

...*Into the* ***Future***

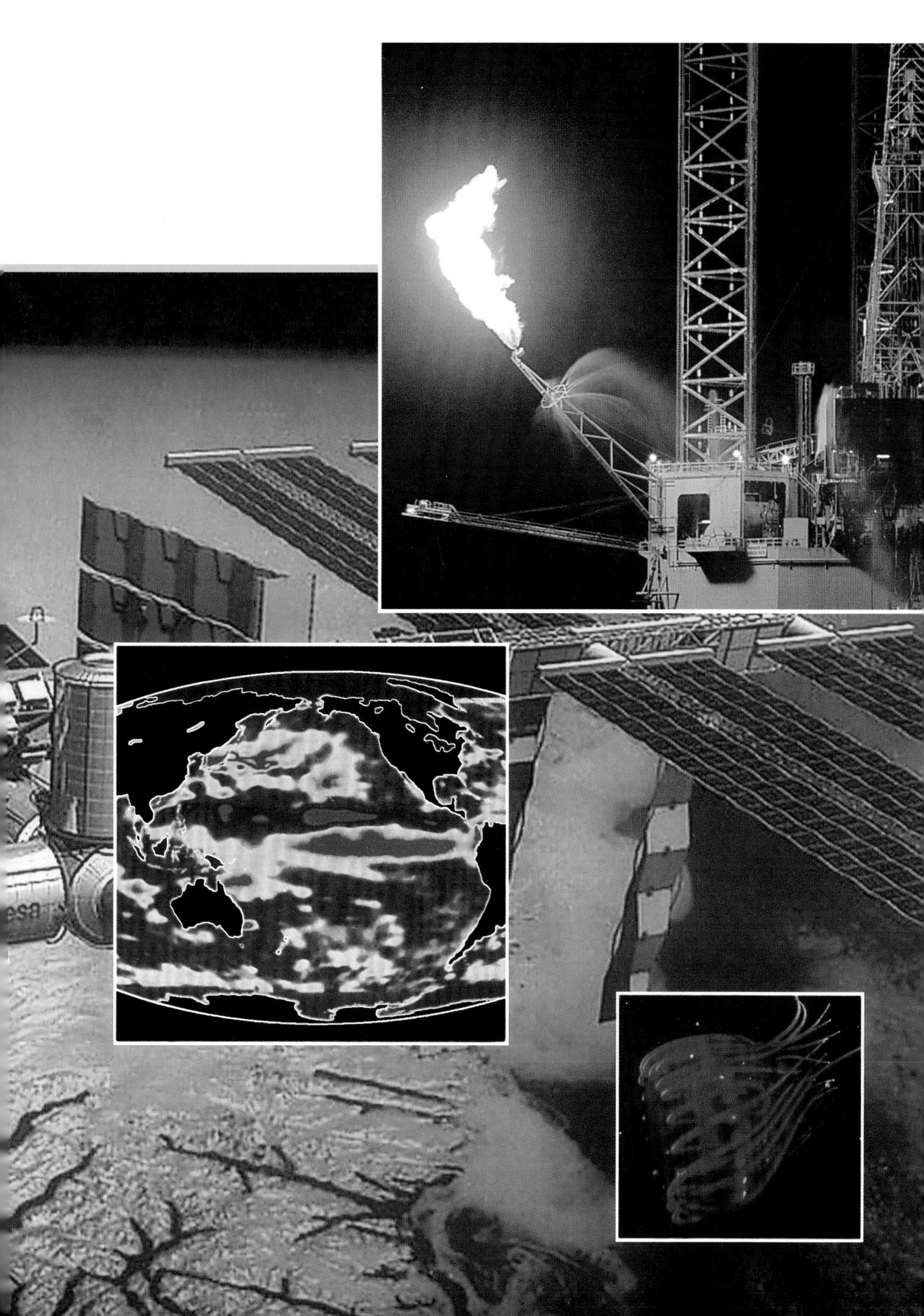

The Sun sometimes has violent electromagnetic storms that move through space. These solar storms can disrupt communications to Earth and damage space equipment. Soon, space weather reports, based on information from satellites and space vehicles, will help scientists control the damage caused by solar storms.

Deep-sea exploration. The ocean is being explored more than ever before to meet the growing needs of the oil, drug, and telecommunications industries. Submarines will still be needed, but robots and remote-controlled craft will do most of the work. More accurate deep-sea maps, made with the help of computers, will make it easier for researchers to locate areas of interest on the ocean floor.

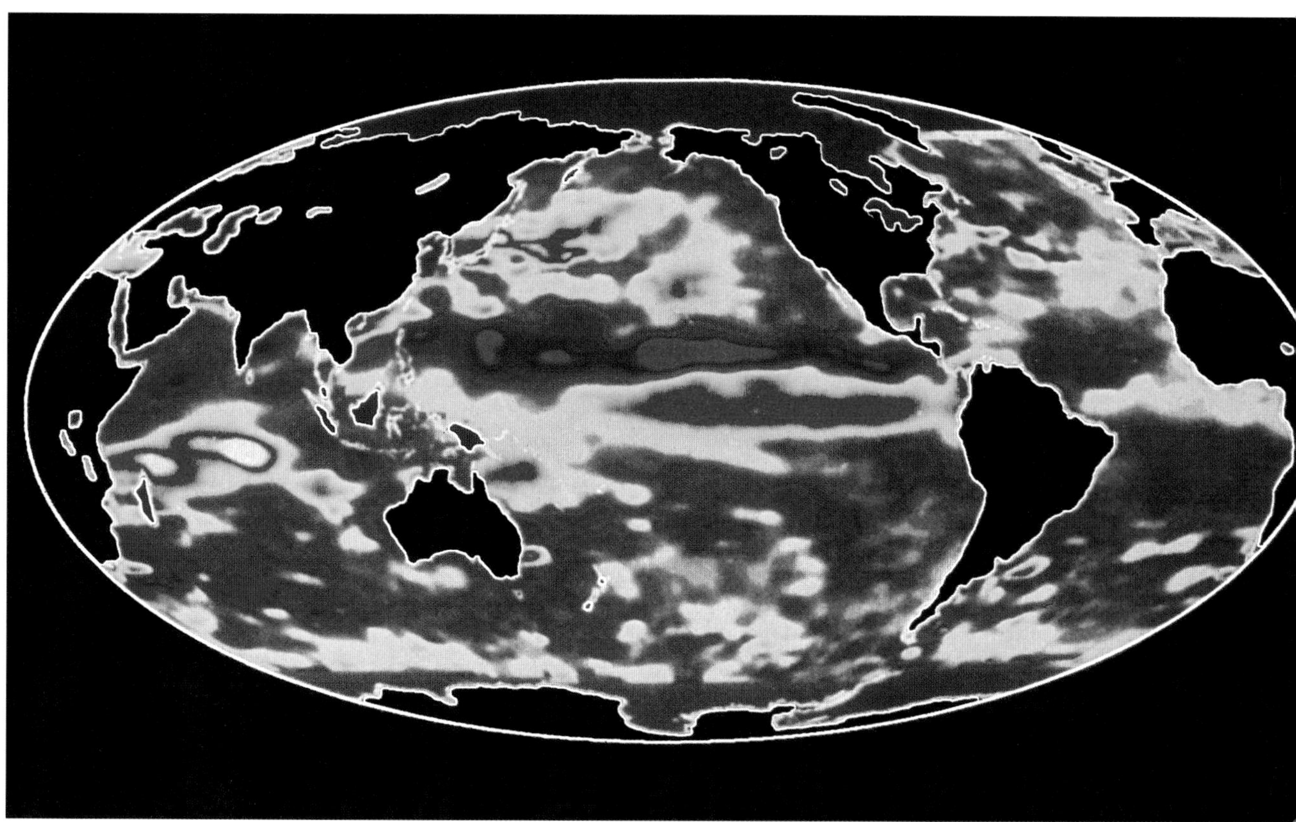

As the world's need for energy grows and sources become harder to find, oil companies will explore deeper waters in search of oil and gas. They will build ultra-deepwater wells 8,000 to 10,000 feet (2,400 to 3,050 m) deep and use new technologies to locate, drill, and process the resources quickly and more efficiently.

Information gathered by satellites in Earth's orbit will help scientists study global climate changes. They will learn how changes in ocean currents, the atmosphere, and global temperature will eventually effect the planet and its ecosystems.

Super weather reports.
New powerful supercomputers, which perform 690 billion calculations per second, will help improve the accuracy of weather forecasts. These computers build complex weather models based on data about Earth's temperature, wind, amount of precipitation (such as rain- or snowfall), and the pressure in the atmosphere. These models will also help forecasters better predict weather emergencies, such as storms and flooding.

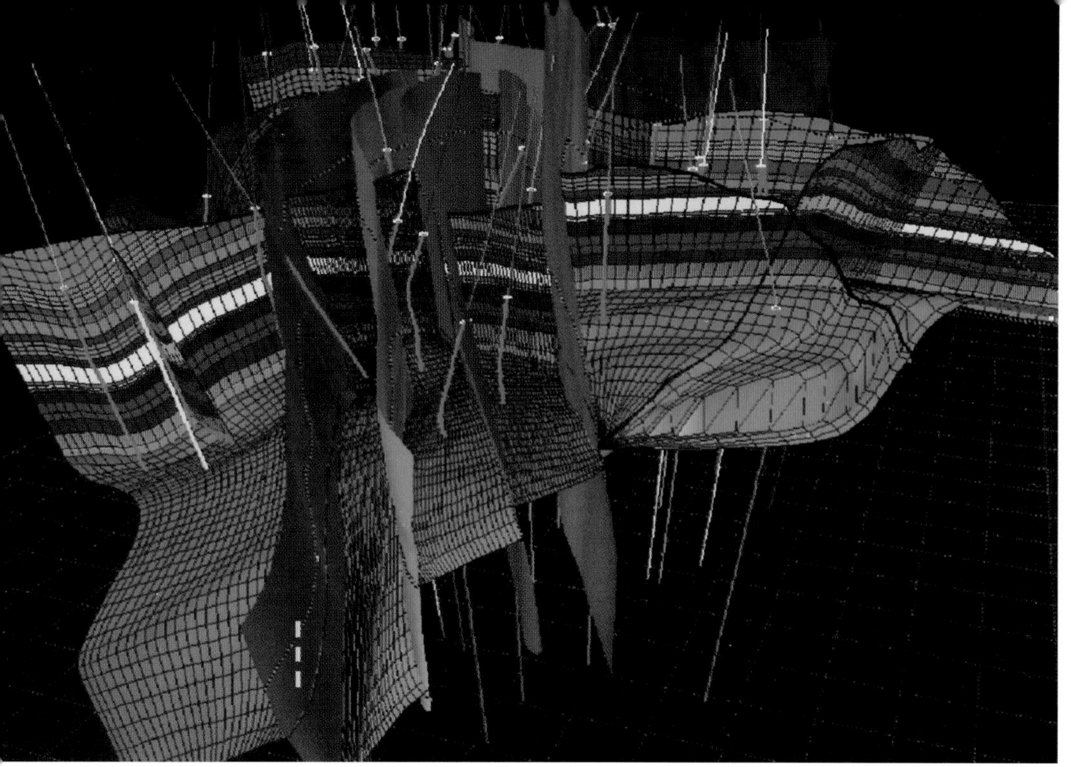

Deep-Earth quakes.
Scientists will explore the deep interior of Earth with new computer software designed for the science of seismology. Seismology is the study of the natural or man-made vibrations in the Earth. This new technology will help scientists build digital models of deep-Earth activities (above). Scientists want to learn more about the boundary between Earth's solid mantle (covering) and its hot, liquid core, which is 1,700 miles (2,735 km) beneath the surface. They hope to understand the movements of the plates of the Earth's crust, which cause earthquakes.

International Space Station.
By 2004, astronauts and cosmonauts will have completed construction of the International Space Station. U.S. space shuttles and Russian rockets will make 45 launches to get the 100 components into Earth's orbit. The pieces will then be assembled in space. The space station will serve as a long-term, orbiting research laboratory. Sixteen countries are participating in the project.

Touring space.
Engineers are developing new, cheaper, reusable space vehicles. These vehicles will be able to take off and land in the same way that airplanes do. With these vehicles, scientists will be able to conduct more space research—and people will be able to vacation in space. In a few years, space tourists may be able to spend up to three days aboard an orbiting cruise ship or longer periods in an orbiting space hotel.

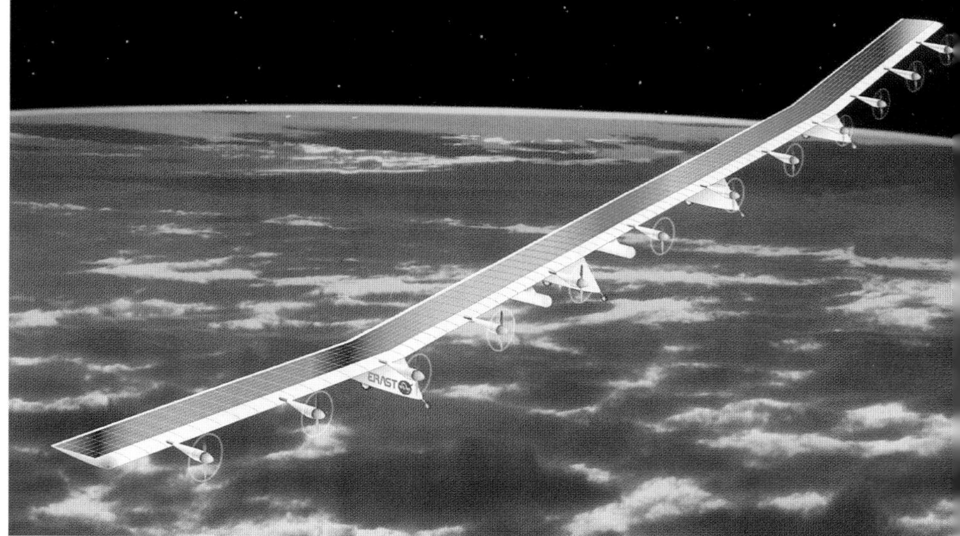

Solar aircraft.
Ultralight airplanes powered by the sun may take over many of the tasks now performed by expensive satellites. The National Aeronautics Space Administration (NASA) hopes to create a fleet of high-altitude, long-endurance solar aircraft to study Earth's weather and atmosphere and to provide telecommunication services. "Flying wings" will be powered by solar cells spread across their upper surface. Solar-powered test planes have already made successful flights as high as 80,000 feet (24,000 m). NASA is setting new goals of 100,000 feet (30,500 m) and higher.

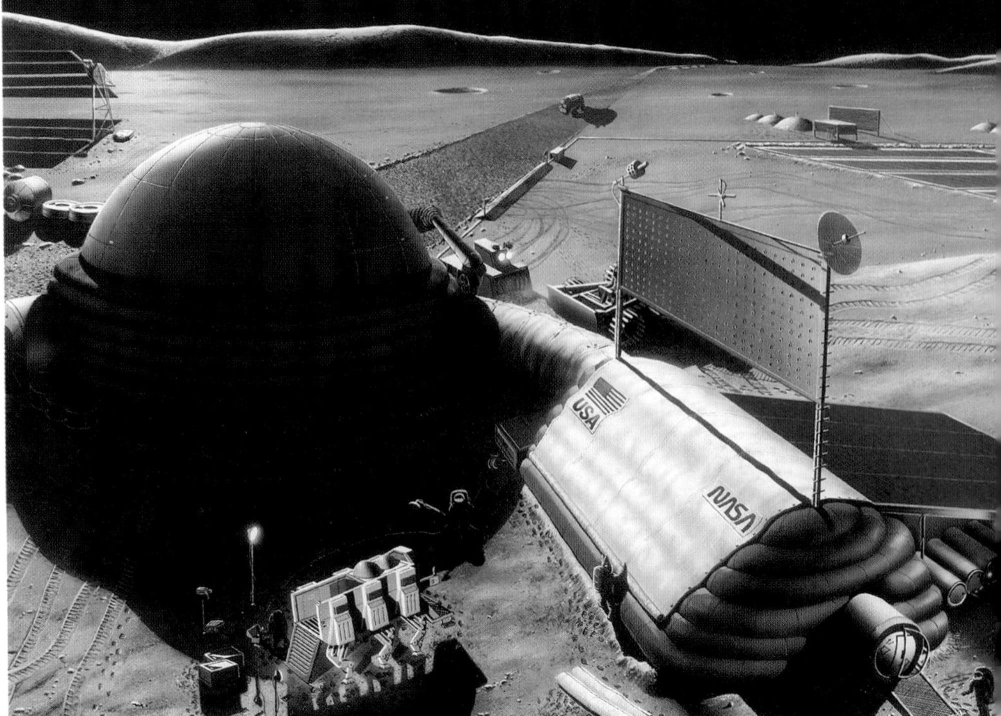

Moon colonies.
Scientists have discovered ice in the soil of the Moon. By heating the soil, they hope to recover liquid water. By reducing the water to its elements—hydrogen and oxygen—they hope to produce air, which would allow humans to breathe in space. A moon colony, in which people could live and work, would serve as a laboratory and as a center for missions to other planets. Scientists believe that it may also be possible to support human life on Mars.

Space mines.
Mining of the Moon, asteroids, and planets may provide materials that are in short supply on Earth. Asteroids, for example, may contain precious metals such as platinum and gold. Iron and nickel could be mined and refined in space to build structures there. The mining may be done by people working in space colonies (settlements) or by robots.

Unmanned deep-space probes will explore the edges of our solar system and beyond. They will send back to Earth the detailed information that they gather as they visit—and, in some cases, land on—asteroids, planets, and comets.

Undersea life.
Undersea life forms may provide important information that will help scientists develop medicines and useful proteins for humans. Scientists are searching for new communities of the strange organisms that live around hot-water vents (currents) on the deep-sea floor. These organisms thrive in harsh chemicals and water as hot as 230° F (110° C).

An orbiting, space-based telescope has been designed to look outside our solar system for planets that may support life. This telescope, called an interferometer, has several separate mirrors that orbit as a unit. It will be able to detect signs of life by analyzing the infrared light given off by distant planets.

Search for life.
Scientists are using powerful radio telescopes to search for signs of intelligent life in the universe. These instruments gather radio signals around stars that are within 200 light-years (about 5.9 trillion miles or 9.5 trillion km) of Earth. Scientists believe that these signals may be communications from civilizations in other solar systems. Computers process the radio signals, alerting scientists when they need to make further studies.

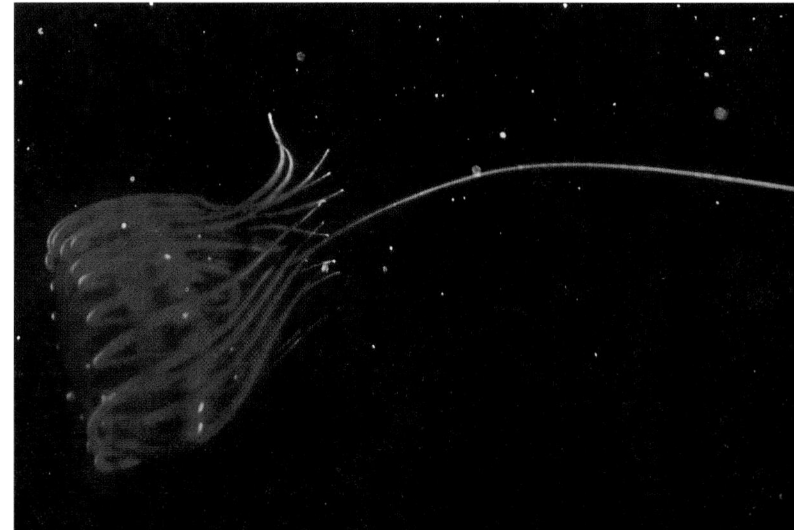

Index

For further reading

Books

Fritz, Jean. Illustrated by Anthony Bacon Verdi. *Around the World in a Hundred Years: From Henry the Navigator to Magellan.* New York: G. P. Putnam's Sons, 1994.

Into the Ice: the Story of Arctic Exploration. Illustrated by Lynn Curlee. Boston: Houghton Mifflin, 1998.

Mason, Antony, and Keith Lye (contributor). *The Children's Atlas of Exploration: Follow in the Footsteps of the Great Explorers.* Brookfield, Conn.: The Millbrook Press, 1993.

Stefoff, Rebecca. *Women of the World: Women Travelers and Explorers.* New York: Oxford University Press, 1994.

Web sites

National Aeronautics and Space Administration

Gives extensive coverage of space exploration
http://nasa.gov

National Geographic

For information on different parts of the world
http://www.nationalgeographic/kids/index.html